A Life in Rhymes

By MC Midlife

Never Be Done

David A. Butler

Hilltop

An imprint of Grackle Publishing, LLC
gracklepublishing.com

Written and illustrated by David A. Butler

Copyright © 2026 David A. Butler
All rights reserved.

ISBN: 978-1-951620-29-5

No part of this publication may be reproduced, distributed, or transmitted in any form or by any means, including photocopying, recording, or other electronic or mechanical methods, without the prior written permission of the publisher, except in the case of brief quotations embodied in critical reviews and certain other noncommercial uses permitted by copyright law. For permission requests, write to grackle@gracklepublishing.com.

To those who gave a positive push

CS, KG, NLSUCKR, MJ, ME, BMX, Levey's Hill, DB, RUSH, Neil Peart, Nena, the Master of Puppets to The Lion and the Cobra, 420 and that first Trip, Mr. Smith—the best gym teacher a kid could ask for, Dropping in, Mamma and Climber, and the East Brigade (you know who you are). Some of us are still Searching For Chin…ru in? Like Suicidal Tendencies said, "We are possessed to sk8!" Dust Bowl going strong and 4th St. Also a special thanks to Mamma C, cared for me more than most, and your meatballs… FORGHEDABOUTIT!

Thank you, and thanks to all the good ones who helped guide and shape this life so far. Until the next…

Table of Contents

YOUTH — 1

   Smokin' a bone — 3

   Flagging — 5

   SPOON — 9

   V. A. T. O. — 12

   Drug PSA — 15

   Migraine — 17

   Women — 19

INSIDE OUT — 21

   Why skateboarding's not a crime… — 23

   The Brain — 27

   90% — 29

   Bipolar Bear — 31

   In my Head — 32

   Frustration — 34

   My Cure — 36

A TOUCH OF FAME — 37

   Manic — 39

   Eminem — 41

   Em2 — 43

   Deep Irish Red — 45

   CPF — 47

   Sign of the Times — 48

PERSPECTIVE 51

Keep it going 53

Toonin' 57

Tick tock tick 58

Fleeting 59

Foreword

To be honest, I'm not sure I can consider this book a book. It's just a collection of thoughts about my life that I put into rhymes. I've dabbled in a variety of art from cartooning to sculpture, but that stuff was tangible.

As I got older, I knew I had to put all these rhymes I had stored in my head down on paper or get to an open mic night somewhere and let them out. I didn't want to take them with me, so I figured I'd share them. Why not?

So here are twenty years of rhymes from the time when I was eighteen until today. Through life's ups and downs, these rhymes tell my story: *A Life in Rhymes.*

— MC MidLife

YOUTH

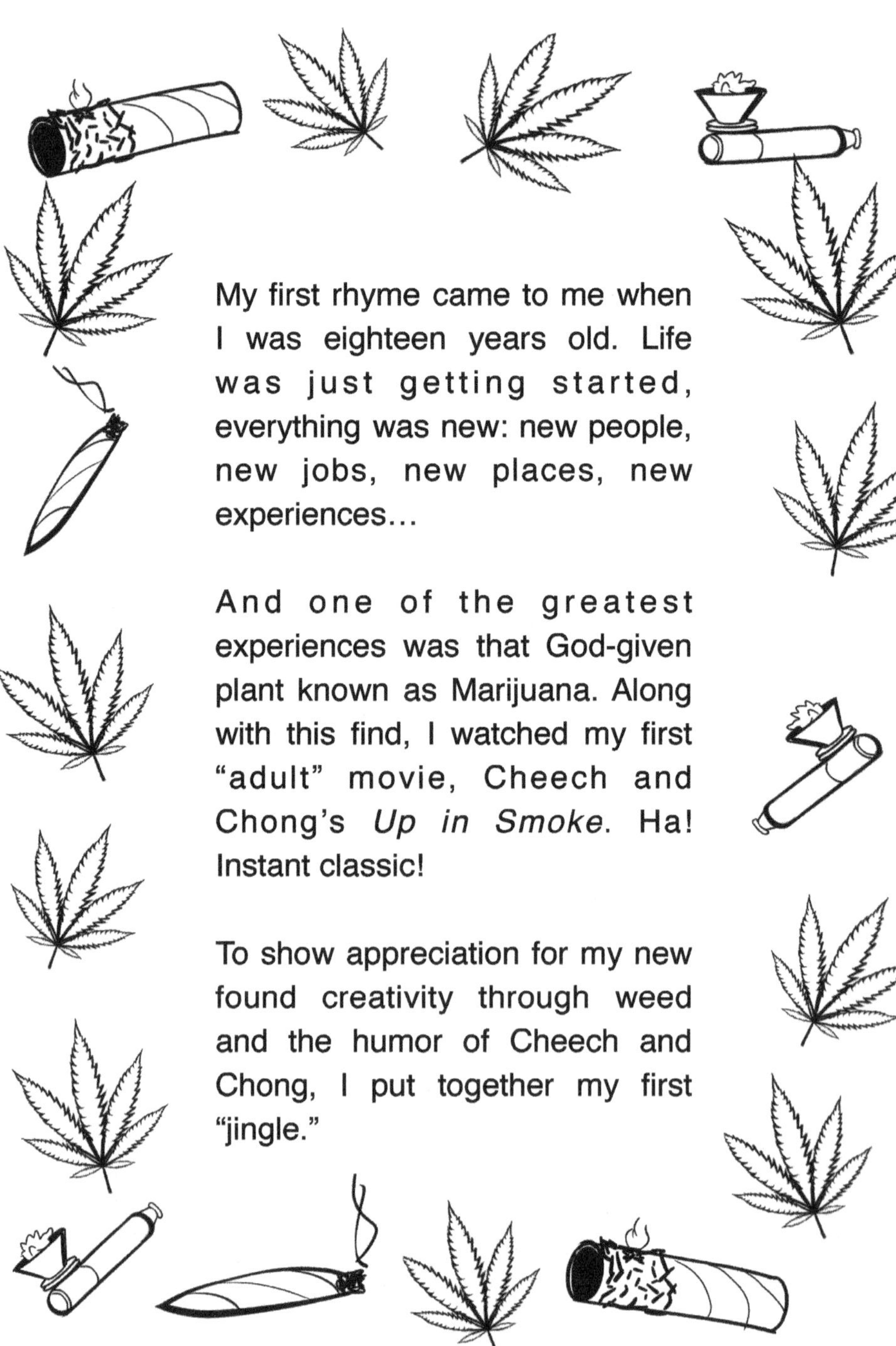

My first rhyme came to me when I was eighteen years old. Life was just getting started, everything was new: new people, new jobs, new places, new experiences...

And one of the greatest experiences was that God-given plant known as Marijuana. Along with this find, I watched my first "adult" movie, Cheech and Chong's *Up in Smoke*. Ha! Instant classic!

To show appreciation for my new found creativity through weed and the humor of Cheech and Chong, I put together my first "jingle."

Smokin' a bone

Walking down the street and I'm smoking a bone.
Each step becomes lighter as I start to zone…
My destination's… home.
Did I mention I was smoking a bone?
Smokin' a bone, smokin' a bone.
Pretty soon I'm gonna be stoned.
Smokin' a bone, smokin' a bone.

Well now I'm at home and no longer zonin',
I think it's about time to roll another bone and
all of a sudden I hear a moanin'.
I look down, my dog is foamin' at the mouth…

Well does it have rabies or is it having babies?
To tell you the truth, man, it won't even phase me
'cause if she was having babies… she's a HE!

Even that won't bother me 'cause I'm
smokin' a bone, smokin' a bone.
Pretty soon I'm gonna be stoned.
Smokin' a bone, smokin' a bone.

You don't like it, leave me alone.
If I offend you, well go the hell home 'cause now I'm
smokin' a bone alone in my home.

Don't take mine, man, get your own!
Smokin' a bone, smokin' a bone.
Pretty soon we're gonna be stoned.
Smokin' a bone, smokin' a bone.
Smokin' a bone.

The rhymes come when they come. I usually don't plan them unless I'm asked to make one. It could be a couple years between rhymes; they're usually tied to a life issue or experience.

In my early twenties, I got a job with Spoon Construction out of Ambler, PA. Great company, great family. Being new to construction, I was put on the flagging crew.

Back then, Bell of PA was still a thing and we would work out in Kennett Square, the mushroom capital of the world. Some days, you're flagging on stretches of road that go for miles… and no cars in sight, just cornfields on the right and cornfields on the left.

Sometimes, the only thing to come down the road is a loose pig or cow. As you're standing there for hours, you have a lot of me time lol… nothing but thoughts… so I had time to rhyme.

<u>Flagging</u>

Flagging construction, man, am I beat.
You think it's easy? Tell it to my feet.
These pups are achin' like bacon.
It's zero below, and I'm shaking.

I can't complain when it's state wages we're making
(which is never), but flagging construction, man, is no joke.
Those cars are coming, you gotta have hope
that the driver's alert and not on dope.
You think they care for you? All I'll say is nope.

'Cause flagging construction is not as easy as it seems.
We gotta put up with @$$holes, you know what I mean.
People that are driving are usually late for work
and if you hold them up, they'll think you're a jerk.

But that's the price they pay for getting up late.
With drivers like this, they're temping our fate.
But when we see them coming, we'll stand up straight
and we'll hold our ground until it's too late.

'Cause that's our job to try to protect,
and that's why we get that big ol' check.
So next time you see a flagger, wave hello,
follow their commands and drive real slow.

Early Morning On Rt. 202, Traffic Slows Towards A Construction Site. Thanks To The Flaggers Who Keep The Irate And Already Late To Work Drivers Moving Smoothly And On Their Way, . .
Well, . . Almost.
Beep
Beep
Honk!
You CK??
Boom
Boom
Boom
Boom
No! There's One more Coming. . . and at That Speed, . . It can Only Be One
click
no brakes
introducing Mr. No Brakes
with music blasting,...
Yeah yeah yeah More speed More speed
Shirt
Faster! Faster! where's the speed That I am After?, . .

BOOM
BOOM
Faster! Faster! I cross the Centerline!,
WITH A QUICK CHANGE ..
Don't Worry,.
WOOSH!
I'll Stop Him
ITS CRASHMAN!
As the Egomaniac poses for fans,..
and in 3, 2, 1
WHAM

As I was on a roll, I wanted to create a rhyme for that same construction company, my second attempt at jingle writing, a nod to my employer and fellow workers.

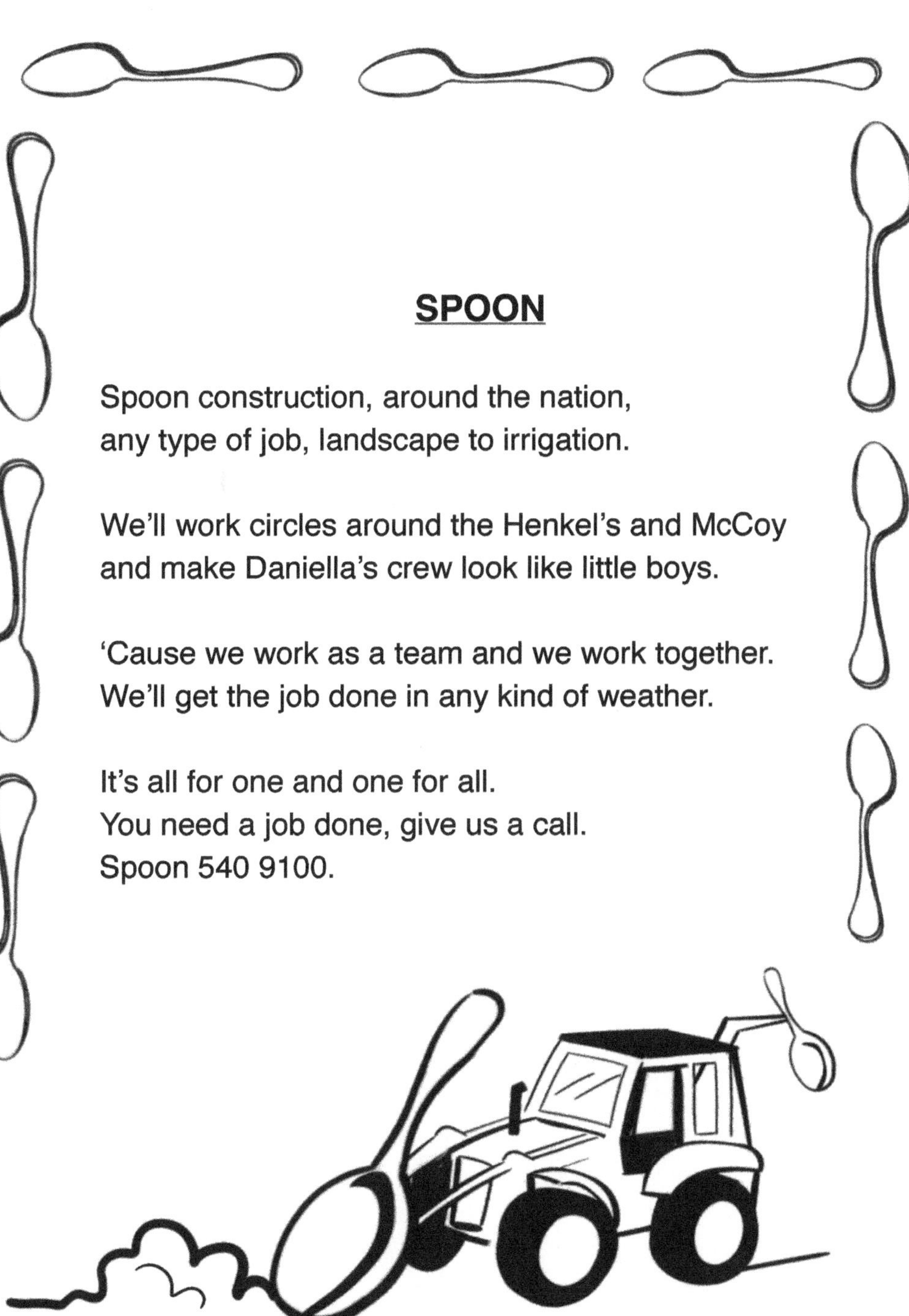

SPOON

Spoon construction, around the nation,
any type of job, landscape to irrigation.

We'll work circles around the Henkel's and McCoy
and make Daniella's crew look like little boys.

'Cause we work as a team and we work together.
We'll get the job done in any kind of weather.

It's all for one and one for all.
You need a job done, give us a call.
Spoon 540 9100.

Have you ever wondered where all those chocolate bunnies come from at Easter?

JUST
WIPE
IT

I think it was the early 90s. It might have been the first one in Philly, not sure… Earth Day. A big event in the city with vendors and an all-day concert. I learned very little about the environment, but I learned a lot about people lol…

As we were entering the grounds, walking forward with a hundred other people, a guy came toward us, saying, "'Shrooms, opium doses … 'Shrooms, opium doses." I was like wow, out in the open, he didn't care. He just wanted to share lol… that was an eye-opening day. Good times…

But back to the environment, I wanted to try an acronym: take a word and break it up. I must of grabbed the idea from a rap I heard. I was a big fan of rap in the 80s and 90s, everything from Grandmaster Flash to Run-DMC. LL was rocking *Bells* and Dougy had *6 Minutes*.

I thought I'd test my "rapping" skills and make an acronym. As you can see, I didn't try to make a complicated word that would be cool to break down, no, no... it's literally a four letter word.

My friends and I would greet each other with, "Yo, sup Vato?" We adopted it from watching Cheech in his movies… anyway… Vato was the word I chose, so here goes…

V. A. T. O.

Very Anxious and Totally Original,
Vato's the name and no, I'm no criminal.
I'm here in peace at least to decease the beast
and then we'll feast on the freedom that we gain
through our hardships and our pain.

But don't you sweat and don't you fear,
to save the planet, this is clear…
some was done in '91, still more to do in '22 —
it's a group effort, all of you!

Worldwide interaction,
no time for maxin' 'n relaxin',
no addition, only subtraction of our lives
if we don't come together,
unless you're content with having bad weather.

So listen up to what I'm saying,
'cause if you don't, pretty soon you'll be praying.
Take time out to read the signs,
yeah, I'm talking the sign of the times.

The world we live in is getting worse,
slowly decreasing is the value of the earth.
Before you get married and think about birth,
think about your kids and what their lives will be worth.

If you want your children to grow with blue skies,
listen to me, you better open your eyes.
Open your eyes and your mind to the sky,
and keep it blue until the day you die,

and that goes double for the green.
We need to seed the weed. Period.

Keep the oxygen in the air, and don't you ever dare not care
about the shit we use and put in the air,
'cause DDT outlawed, PCB outlawed and should be banned,
and that's one way to save the land.

Next on the list are the seas and the oceans,
se se se seas and the oceans,
they need to be saved.
I'll tell you over. I'll tell you over and over.
I'll tell you over and over until it's engraved
in your head and your mind.

We gotta act now 'cause we're running out of time.
So like I said before, we need action, no relaxin'.
These words I speak are all mother FKN Facts son.

So I've given you some knowledge, so use it, don't abuse it.
This world's the only one we got, so let's just do it.

A little goofy in retrospect…

This next one, the only thing I knew about the drug or alcohol world was from TV movies or the news, so as I tried to make a friendly PSA about drugs, this is the outcome…idk kinda works.

<u>Drug PSA</u>

You losers that deal probably think it's grand,
chillin' with your ladies and feeling like a man,
money to burn and caviar to eat,
but sooner or later you're gonna cheat.

On your own supply so you could get high,
but once is all 'cause next you'll be in juvenile hall
for your robbing, your stealing, your mugging, your killing
for those few dollars so you could get ON…

Listen up to the rest of my song.

Look at your life, it's a wreck, you're a mess.
I think it's about time that you confess
to God Almighty, tell him your sins,
ask for forgiveness and new days to begin.

But now you're addicted and you can't get away…
the Betty Ford clinic is where you're gonna stay.

So yeah, it kinda works, little dated…

This next one is dedicated to all those who know and suffer with migraines.

It's funny, when I was young, I always thought people were faking, making up a name because they had a headache lol. I'm like just take an Advil and go back to work.

Little did I know, bunch of years later, BAM, I'm now a member. With that, anyone out there that might be skeptical of migraine suffers, trust me, to not know is a gift. Just wish them well and be glad it's not you, 'cause…

<u>Migraine</u>

Shut the lights, close the blinds,
what the fuck is wrong with my mind.

Eye strain, pain in the brain,
feels like my skull can't contain, going insane…

Is this what they call a migraine?

Fuck that shit, grab a blade,

cut a vein, tie me down in front of a train,
a hundred lashes with a cane,
forget the chute and leave the plane,
do anything to avoid the pain.

Is that enough? Can I refrain?
Or you need more examples of our strain?

When it comes, it's like a hurricane,
pressure builds, grab a drill,
drill a hole, make a drain,
do anything to ease the pain.

Your life's constrained,
you live in vain.
To live like this is inhumane…

That's what it's like to have a migraine.

So yeah, luckily for me, I found my trigger, so I pretty much avoid them. Anyone who suffers, Gbless, look for your trigger and good luck.

I believe this next one came to me around eighteen. Just started dating and was surrounded by women all day at work. And at this time, if someone had asked me, "Hey kid, what do you think about women?" I would of said…

<u>Women</u>

Every guy has a type he likes,
some like Sugar and some like Spice.
And even though, guys,
they think we're never right,
having someone close is kind of nice.

But women have a power you can't describe.
Yeah, WE know when it's time to hide from our honeys
who are always bright and sunny,
and never once try to make us feel like a dummy
in public, no doubt.
You don't know what it's about.
You try to calm her down, then she only starts to shout.

Once feeling good, now your feeling small,
to make matters worse, you're standing in the mall.
People are staring and she's still swearing…
About what? Are you kiddin'?
We're talking about women.

Haha, that's funny, that's beautiful, my first take on women.

Where to go from here?

INSIDE OUT

Well, I think these next few I can group together as a look into my brain, my thoughts and struggles in life. And honestly, I guess, depending on your life circumstances, we get a better understanding of ourselves, our brain, our chemical make up, and an understanding of our upbringing and those around us. Unfortunately, you live half your life and go through some shit to figure it all out.

Growing up, there was definitely not as many initials as there are today. Personally, I think general practitioners don't know, since they're not really versed and just throw out words to see if something sticks: ADD, OCD, anxiety disorder, depressive disorder. Here, try this med, oh no, wait, try this one, never knowing, just hoping…

Anyway, like I said in the opening, this is just my experience and thoughts on life. Unfortunately, it is so true that it is all about the story you tell yourself. Not realizing it until later, I wrote a rhyme describing myself in misery, and because the rhyme sounded good, I repeated it almost every day because I like the way it flowed. I repeated it to myself over and over again because it rhymed and worked. But as I was reliving those words every time I rhymed, I was programming myself to live that story. Crazy, right? It's amazing what you learn when you open your conscience to the universe and learn a whole new understanding of yourself. You'll see what I mean in a minute. So like I said, these next few are dedicated to all those who have struggled in one way or another with the mental side of life and might be just a little touched. ;)

Ollie on a dime Method

Am I a sociopath, a psychopath,
a schizophrenic who thinks too fast,
a manic depressive who can't find his path,
or just a skater who fell on his ass,
broke some ribs and now has to gasp?

Me quit skating, don't make me laugh,
it's the only time I don't think of the past.
Skating, creating, totally focused
on the moves I'm making
instead of the thoughts that keep on taking:
anger, remorse, anxiety,
STOP!

Grab the board, take that ollie and pop.
It frees your mind, slows down time.

For as you know, you have to focus to grind.
Push through the vert and fly to the sky,
slide the rail, slap some tail
and wait for thrasher to come in the mail.

Grosso had it right, giving love to the beast.
It's because of skateboarding, now I have peace.

Air on a dare Too much air

Have you seen him Ollie

kind and rewind

ain't enoughPlease be

Ah yes, the brain... what a gift, unknowingly.

If you're considered a "normal" human, on a daily basis, you don't even think about most processes because those actions become wired-in through repetition.

The brain is a complicated construct capable of incredible things.

The Brain

The brain, the brain, not one's the same,
some are born striving, others born crying,
others insane…

We push and pull to try to figure ourselves out,
but collateral damage is done, no doubt.
You see it in nature with the runt of the litter,
if you're not strong or quick, you don't get dinner.

So we test ourselves as we grow,
we test our limits, we test the word "no,"
but some don't manage their damage,
as they pick on others to prove their worth.

What you thought was innocent, what you thought was a joke,
was now a lifetime insult and a loss of hope.
The brain, the brain, not one's the same,
did you get to pick it, choose it or give it a name?

Chances are you got what you got,
and if it's not a lot, you got what you got.

So we make do with what you gave us, how you made us,
what you've instilled and engrained in us.
It's your thoughts and actions that shape us,
it's through your words that you frame us.

So you should probably refrain from us
because you're creating little bastards
who couldn't care if they were dust.

This one is an example of the story you tell yourself. I think this one came about sometime in my mid to late twenties.

It's probably not a story you should tell yourself every day. Even if there's no ill will, you're confirming something every time you speak.

Long.

Lesson.

Learned.

<u>90%</u>

90% of the time, I'm this guy,
the wrong guy,
the wrong me to control you,
the wrong us to control we,
to make us do things we don't wanna do.

On further exam, my brain's blistered,
like that mutant rat, I'm Splintered,
injured and withered,
thoughts fractured, scattered and backwards,
held captive by the insane raptor,
scratching and clawing his way through his laughter,
over my disaster; he's an evil little bastard…

Hey! Dave here,
escaping the brain here,
not sure how long I can remain here,
stay here,
always gotta check the rear for the mad puppeteer,
looks clear.

See I'm the one that likes to have fun,
the innovative one,
the creative one,
the one that's passionate and gets things done.
Oh crap,
here he comes…

Back in your hole,
know your role,

your thoughts, your actions I control,
your dreams, ambitions, black rabbit hole.

Personality disorder?
…uh, no,
everything seems in order…
your compulsions are excessive,
your attention's deficient,
your depression's manic,
and you're an empathetic schizophrenic…

So how can you say disorder
when disorder's been the only order?
hahaha hahaha hahaha hahaha hahaha.

Oh, what a mess is, his head is,
I'd hate to see him without his medicine.
It saves the day, it keeps me at bay,
but those days he can't take…
mmmyum! What can I say?

He's primed for the taking.
Make no mistaking,
he's a week away without taking…
Monday, Tuesday, Wednesday,
here I come,
Thursday, Friday, Saturday.

Let's have some fun…
Back n forth pacing,
mind ever racing,
negative thoughts in his head, overtaking.

I keep on pressing,
but he's not yet breaking.
He can have the battles,
it's the war I'm taking.

Bipolar Bear

You don't understand the bipolar bear,
first you scare, poke, then stare,
never understanding the storms in there.

Take their meds and I'll get there.

I gotta take meds and that's not fair.

See, what you see, you don't see,
and what you see, I don't see.

All this time, trapped in my mind,
thinking I was normal but way offline.

Was the fault mine for my mind?

I'm a chemical mixture past its prime,
all this time trapped in my mind.

Life is my sentence
but it's also my crime.

That last one was another story I told myself over, over, and over again, not realizing the affects…

This next one flows well, sounds good, has a good ending, and I would spit it every day to myself because I liked the way it sounded. Remember, it's the story you tell yourself, pay attention to it. The 90% story was over twenty years ago. I made this one five years ago. It's crazy some things have changed but the story stayed the same.

In my Head

I'm in my head but out of my mind.
Should I lay on the couch to see what we find?
I've been played, set up, tricked, maligned.
Or is that just my state of mind?

But I am an intuitive mastermind.
All I'm looking for is peace of mind,
something here I could never find.

So is any time a fine time to pass the time
in your downtime with stories of past times?
Or is that too many rhymes of past times causing a paradigm…

Huh?
See, sometime in the meantime been a long time
waiting on Showtime starting in no time.

A friend of mine has his own paradigm.
He's a should have been, a could have been,
had the skills to explode but he never pulled the pin.

What a sin, look at him,
always went to work but that never worked for him.
Where to start, how to begin…

Has he always been a has been,
from the jump never to win,
cards stacked against him all the way back to conception?

Conception, perception,
yeah they probably could have used protection,
self-reflection, inspection,
humans to him are the infection.

Spending billions on parents' obsession for perfection,
every kid needs a session,
so we can make our corrections.
It's either ADD, OCD or depression,
so let's just medicate and up the rate until they pay attention.

A total dissection of natural selection,
roads below paved with these intentions.
So that begs the question: is life the test or the lesson?
Was class in session? How's your retention?
Did you take notes and pay attention?

Why the tension? Did I fail to mention
my way of thinking is from the fourth dimension?

I think this one came about earlier in life, probably early twenties. You're starting out, first apartment, first independence, then the bills start coming. Things need fixing, responsibilities are increasing, it's your first overwhelming experience of adulting.

Frustration

It's not allowed, it's forbidden, it's prohibited, no kiddin'.
Get banned, get declined, get refused all the time.
Got a request, they'll reject it; need a callback, forget it.
Get turned down, turned around, one way, wrong way,
trying to get ahead, not your day.

But don't worry, they still need you, they need you to bleed you,
they gotta make their take, increase their rates.
They'll charge you for weight, they'll charge you for freight,
meanwhile you work two jobs just to fill your plate.

It's still not enough, so where's your break…
They'll push more papers across their desk,
"Sign right here, we'll relieve that stress."
HaHaHa, laugh out loud, they took the bait;
now it's too late, that fine print said *Triple the Rate*!

Now take your stress and triple the weight,
nothing but fees filling your plate,
now your bills are gonna be late,
what's your fate, filling with hate.
Turn the other cheek they preach. That's great.

What's gonna happen when I run out of cheeks,
like Rocky said, it's a kick in the teeth.
I'm out of cheeks and out of teeth,
I should probably go to church 'cause I'm losing belief.

I'm not in Seattle but I'm losing sleep,
like Dave Mustaine, everyday's the same,
just getting by with the *Skin o' My Teeth*.

I look back through the mirror in disbelief.
My life's ground chuck.
I'm Charlie Brown,
good grief.

My Cure

I've turned depression on its ass,
what used to be a curse is now a gift.

Its my job to cry, so others don't have to…
It's my job to feel sorrow, so others can soar…
It's my job to be unlovable, so others can be loved.

What used to give me anger, the fact that I'm depressed,
now gives me pause and time to reflect…

Because at the low point, when the rain starts to flow,
the pain I feel, is so someone else never knows…

If that's my gift, then let me keep giving.
It's an easy trade so others keep living.

A TOUCH OF FAME

Okay, enough with the downtrodden re livin', let's have some fun…

I'm not sure, maybe I got the idea from Eminem, but I wanted to challenge myself to write a rhyme that I could spit really, really fast and still have it be understood and make sense, kind of like that commercial when we were kids for Micro Machines race cars.

With that, I open the challenge to you all. My fastest time for this one is ten seconds. Go for it…

Manic

My rhymes are manic, panicked and erratic.
If if spit them any faster, it'll probably cause static,
like an M16 goes Ratatattatat
to the cat and the hat switch TatatatRatat,
you rat pack addict in the attic in a panic,
same cat with the habit that framed Roger Rabbit.
Or has the Force awakened…
and you're just an AT-AT at it.

See, we can have fun. Did you try, did you beat ten seconds? It's fun to talk that fast, isn't it?

Oh, speaking of Eminem, I forget the year, it was early in the social media explosion, and I figured why not, send him a rhyme to see what he thought, never thinking I'd hear back.

A day or so later, I got a response. He said, "Yo, go check out my latest album… blah blah blah," and then he wrote, "Not bad."

I don't know about you, but I got a "Not bad" from Eminem!

I'll take it! Think I'm gonna put that on my tombstone: "How was life? Not bad." So I'm taking that as a compliment and gonna believe that's cool as shit. So here is my shout-out to Em.

Eminem

Yo Em, where ya been…
still in the lab with the paper and pen,
just hanging out with your family and friends?

Either way it's okay,
you've earned your keep,
you've earned your sleep,
you've earned your right to live in peace,
we're just not done sucking your teat.

I'm not berating,
just anxiously waiting,
back and forth pacing,
for your next great creation.

So sing it, bring it, you got a catapult then fling it,
I'm not impatient just patient adjacent.

Shit do you blame us, you made us, in return you famous,
anyway just a fan not named Stan,
waiting on your next jam,
BAM.

It was a little while later, maybe even a couple years, before I made this one and sent it.

Unfortunately, no response this time.

That's okay, I'm still riding high from "Not bad."

Em2

Yo Em,
DB again,
just a friend you don't know,
who you'd probably tell to go blow,
since it's not your job to say hi
to every Tom, Dick and Joe you don't know.

But before you go, you must know,
you reach us, you teach us, you give us a voice,
if you ever quit, that's your choice,
but we'll still be here,
stuck in the muck,
stuck in a rut,
tied in knots from our string of bad luck,
looking for some kind of something… Fuck!

But like you said with *Survival*,
you gotta dig deep when you spiral,
even getting tribal and primal,
and when you make it through… Revival.

I was once friends with two Irish Setters. They were some cool dudes. Here's my shout-out to them. Read it in your best Irish accent.

Deep Irish Red

'Tis an Irish Setter named Clancy
who always strikes the girls' fancy.
He runs and hops and eats lots of carrots,
seems bit mistaken himself as a rabbit…

Then there's the other, his crazy Irish brother,
a very talkative lad who's always a wee bit bad
and never far from sin. It's the deep Irish Red named Finnegan.

By themselves, you can handle,
bring them together, your house will be shambles…
They're majestic at sight and playful with might.
When these lads are resting, aye, that's a good night.

Okay, this next one really pisses me off, and I'm sure it does the same to you. Let's not pretend that the increase in fatalities on the roads isn't due to texting and social media, and the amount of you f#$@ idiots with your phone in your face while driving down the road, FME! Everybody thinks they're impervious…

I snapped. Driving down 95 doing 70, keeping with traffic, I looked over to my right, and this mother fkr had both hands on his phone, not even looking ahead, like what!? You're the reason I can't work a driving job.

I've caught myself on two occasions, inches away from going to prison. I almost ran two mother fkrs off the road for texting and driving, because that innocent family of four, across the intersection, are not gonna die on my watch! I had to take myself off the road professionally. Look for yourself, take a walk one day on one of your roads and watch as people drive by you, and see who has their phone in their face. The amount I saw was disturbing, hopefully maybe one person reads this rhyme, listens, and it helps…

"Okay, here we go, Dick. We're live!"

"That's right, Tom. It's another sad day here in town."

"Do you know the cause, Dick?"

"I do Tom, I do. It was another case of CPF."

"CPF? I can't believe it."

<u>CPF</u>

Modern day Americans, you're a disgrace,
get that fucking cellphone out of your face,
60 down the highway is probably not the place
for your incessant need of value…

CPF was the case. That's Cell Phone Face,
in case you need mace to wake, to come face to face
with the fact you just sealed someone's fate.

(ScreeetchCrash!!)

That last text just took your last breath.
Now you're laid to rest, lives are wrecked,
your family's a mess all because of CPF!

What's it gonna take to change your life,
your mother, your sister, your daughter, your wife?
Grow the fuck up and put the phone down,
everyone's home safe now, how's that sound?
Pay attention to the road and enjoy the ride.
If it's that important, pull to the side.

Stop being selfish, be a little selfless.
It's up to you to be the help or be helpless.
So make a pledge to drive your best
if not for yourself, then think of the rest
and stop another casualty of CPF.

As far as Public Service Announcements go, I think that's a good one. We might have to clean it up a little bit, but I think it sends a good message. Maybe we get it on the radio someday. At least it's out there in some fashion.

It was probably about ten years ago, some friends and I were sitting around a table. Keith, an old school guy from Philly said, "Make me a rhyme about the sign of the times." Accepting the challenge, I gave him my rhyme the following weekend.

<u>Sign of the Times</u>

It's 5 am and they've lit the fuse,
more of us killed, more of us screwed.
This is how they choose to news:
death, destruction, corruption, greed.
This is how we wake up, the first thing we see.
Fuck the news. How can it be?
I'm stressed the fuck out before I pee!

But this is what they want us to see, control what we know,
tell us what we need. Anxiety and fear is all they feed…
Let's keep it going, get out with the hash…
when stock markets crashed, our leaders got rash,
took a dash for our cash, took our stash in a flash.
If they want to make more, they'll just raise more tax.
All this does is make us want to clash, makes us want to bash,
makes us want to do what the Captain said and Hulk Smash!

But let's digress, there's a lot to digest.
Yes, it's true this world's a mess,
and if you obsess, you play life's chess without a vest,
because if you let it consume you, it's like two to the chest.
See life is stress, life is mess,
the ones without problems are the ones laid to rest…

Want some advice? Get a vice,
one that won't control you, own you or take your life.
Find something out there to help you succeed.
I get a boost to my stride from that weed.
It's just a weed that grows in the ground,
turns frowning clown upside down.
In an instant, mood's changing,
thoughts rearranging, mind shifted, spirits lifted.
With nature's gift, now I'm gifted with motivation, inspiration,
innovation for creation. God's gift to the world was this creation.

Now let's change the station, back to the nation,
still there's oppression, deep in recession,
working our way to the next great depression.
Seems we never learn from our lessons,
spending billions of trillions to play on the moon,

meanwhile there's others who can't fill their spoons.
When's their next meal? Never too soon.
This trend continues, society's doomed
to repeat the sins of the past, working two jobs just to get gas.
Meanwhile, we struggle, CEOs get a pass.
You think that we'll settle for this, kiss our ass.

But don't get it twisted, let's understand,
it's ten times worse in these foreign lands.
Iraq, Iran, Afghanistan, Pakistan, livin' in sand,
nothing to do but work on your tan.
Then Taliban destroy the land. Choose the wrong god,
you'll get in the van. Get caught stealing, you'll give 'em a hand.
Blow something up and then you're a man.
That's why WE got the greatest land.

But let's take a look at the United States,
inflation and debt at the highest rate.
We the People will bend, hope we don't break.
How much can we take?
You're always giving promises, give us a break!
Price increases, quality decreases,
sending jobs over seas because it's cheapest.
Is there hope? I say nope.
Go to the Vatican and pray with the Pope.
Prayer must be working, the Lord sent dope,
that magical leaf that lets you cope
with this country's slippery slope.

So search your answers, search your mind,
we gotta get this country back in line.
Let's make a difference, let's rewind
because all this here's been sign of the times.

PERSPECTIVE

This is not what I meant when
I said we needed to soak your foot!

Of course, it is all about perspective. I'm sure if I wrote something today about the sign of the times, it would be a lot different. Either way, kinda works…

Keith liked it. He said, "How did you do that, man?"

I just told him…

<u>Keep it going</u>

I keep it flowing and going,
take any words and start sewing.
My words are seeds that keep growing
from the pages of phrases I'm knowing,
taking my skills and just honing.

You double down, you're just cloning.
Got no reception, start roaming,
but quit your bitchin' and moanin', groaning.
You only live once. You're not Logan.

Life's moving fast, never slowin'.
Take your wishin' and hope'n
and drop that shit like you're Holden.

Know what you want and get goin'.
Work like a dog and start foaming.
Goals and dreams you'll be owning,
so never stop, keep it going.

Don't be Loki and frozen, run your life like you're Odin,
down that path you have chosen
until you reach your goals and you're golden!

Whew, that's a mouth full. Lost my breath on that one… I guess that's part of the reason why I like to rhyme, the challenge to create a well-versed, long-winded sentence lol. I'm sure I'm not the only one out there who's rhymed a time or two in their life, just for kicks, 'cause you caught a rhyme when you were talking, then you took it home and expanded on it. Fun, right? Oh and the Holden part was a nod to my buddy Holden who was a pup in an animal rescue. He was shot and had a bullet close to his spine, so they wouldn't operate, and part of his issue was he couldn't hold his bowels any longer… and he would just drop that $#@! Now when you reread it, you'll know.

Life is crazy and life is amazing, like I said, perspective. Sometimes it's true, you have to bottom out so you can soar. Then you understand the rise of the phoenix that you heard about growing up. I always loved the battle of working out, pushing your body to a limit, feeling the struggle and giving everything to get that bar back on the rack. Winning the battle… and then the badge of honor when you can't move or walk the next day, knowing you pushed it and survived. You are now stronger than you were yesterday… and that's life, and that's literally the solution to most of life's problems. Just treat it like a workout, attack it, push through it, rack it and keep moving…

From time to time, I would look toward various motivational speakers from Tony Robbins to Alan Watts to David Goggins, Jocko Willink and Eric Thomas. For one reason or another, they all hit something in me that keeps me focused, positive and moving forward. Be open to others when it comes to growth, sometimes you'll find a perspective that will change your life. I hope to continue that mindset and leave something positive. If you're just starting out in life, or you've been through it, my message is the same…

Dreams and ambitions start when we are young. Some might call them delusions of grandeur. As we grow, our dreams and goals get solidified as just that, dreams and goals. Life happens, work happens, bills keep coming… so your dreams and goals get put in the closet. You'll get to them later. Right now, you need to take care of all that other crap because you don't have time right now to act on it.

Ha! Ha, I say. *Distraction from action leads to a life of stress full relaxin'.*

So we bust our asses for others all week long for those few hours a week we get to chill. We tell ourselves we've earned it. We kick back on the couch with some dinner, maybe watch a little TV and veg out. Meanwhile, you're looking at the closet and thinking *yeah, someday I'll get to that.* Meanwhile, you're content laying in bed watching TV at the moment… because you earned it.

Hm, what have I earned? A moment in time to keep my dreams on the shelf, a moment in time to keep my goals unattained?

Even though we feel at that moment that we don't have the time or the energy to start pursing something, we are absolutely wrong with this mindset. Yes, It is okay and recommended to take a load off and chill, don't get me wrong, but if you step back, pay attention to your situation, you'll realize that we do actually waste a lot of time just chillin' *because we earned it.*

As I listen to others like Jocko Willink, one of his lessons is no matter how small a movement might be, just take the movement. It got me thinking. If I stand still for a minute, it feels like an eternity. If you test yourself, you can get a lot done in a minute. So, take your chill time and subtract five minutes to pursue you dreams and goals. You've earned it!

It's really that simple, even if that five minutes was opening the closet door, taking out that box, and blowing the dust off. That's it. That's today's progress. Tomorrow, you'll take another baby step, and before you know it, you're achieving something you thought you never would, but you did. You've done it!

Believe in your dreams and goals and never stop reaching, no matter how small a step. What they say is true: your mind doesn't know the difference between what is real and what is fantasy. I've mentioned the brain a couple of times in here and how amazing it is. When we focus on the past or negative aspects of life, we constantly draw that energy toward us and continue to live in that life construct. With that rationale, it seems a little too simple, right?

"Fake it 'til you make it." It's literally that simple. Once you BELIEVE in your goals and dreams, you'll take the steps to achieve. Trust me, when you stay focused on your path, positive things will happen for you… just as the negative things keep happening when you're stuck in the past. With this simple mindset, I have literally changed my life and achieved dreams and goals that have been in the closet for years.

When I was about six years old, I remember my grandfather asking me, as I lay on the floor reading the Sunday comics, "What do you want to do when you grow up?"

This goal/dream started that day.

Toonin'

Toonin', cartoonin', that's what I'll be doin'
for living, for life with two kids and a wife.
A house, a boat, I'll put in a moat
to keep back my goats.

You think this is funny, baaaaaaaaaa… no joke.
I'm going for mine, you're going for yours.
You gotta work hard to get what is yours.
You gotta work hard to keep what you got.
Love what you do and do it a lot.

Understand to be the man it takes a plan to get what you can
out of this game called life with very low strife.
I want to keep winnin' and no longer sinnin'.
Let's take it back to the very beginning.

When it all starts, you can't go Half a Heart.
You gotta keep reaching. That's why I'm preaching.
If you learn one thing, I guess you'll say I'm teaching,
but class is over, class is dismissed.
Ask me a question if there's something you missed.

If you want to move forward, you gotta take that step.
If you don't take the step, then you're gonna regret it.
Never regret and never say what if, 'cause life's too short
to have something you miss.

Tick tock tick

Tick tock tick, it's getting late.
Tick tock tick, it's another new date.
Tick tock tick, it's getting late, getting late,
getting late, getting late…

I'm just waiting on daybreak, for what a difference a day makes,
another day to retake, rewind and replace,
the day before you forsaked, the day before you laid to waste,
left in haste, took your dreams and goals and made them paste.

(Sound effects here, descending boom,
followed by a rooster crowing.)

Now you're awake, you got a fresh slate,
whatcha gonna do to make it great?
How are you going to live above the hate?
Every decision chooses your fate.
You have a fresh start, so recreate,
pull your weight, don't be late.

The man above will take the weight,
so have some faith but do not wait,
don't get distracted by the snakes,
follow those who bend but don't break,
try so hard you cause the earth to quake.
Always give before you take,
go for your goals, get a house on a lake, a 50-year cake,
whatever it takes. Even if it's just a 20-ounce steak,
this movie's yours, make it great!

Tick tock tick, it's getting late…

<u>Fleeting</u>

Life is fleeting, same days repeating. I'll do it later
has no meaning. So move your ass 'cause life goes fast,
before you know it, it's past.

We gotta go, we gotta leave, we gotta bounce, we gotta jet,
a fresh start is waiting, on your marks, get set.
A fresh start can't wait, your life a remake, pull up stakes,
vacate, leave out of this place, leave out, move out, get out and
stay out dead set?

You bet, not yet, don't forget, take chances, play roulette with
the world? with your life! Time to get out and see some sights…
new places and faces, find your oasis, it's a case by case basis,
so break the braces, leave no traces, your life's as big as you
make it, so make it, don't fake it or forsake it, use both hands to
grab it and take it.

There's no limit on your vision so make the decision
to achieve the life you see yourself winnin'… For when we are
young, the world is ours. We can be what we want and reach for
the stars. The decisions you make decide who you are.

Are you living your dreams or living in your car?

See life's an illusion, contusion, optical confusion 'cause how
are there some that can't stop smiling, then two doors down,
others can't stop crying. I'm tired of crying, I'm tired of thinking
about dying, I'm tired of just surviving, I'm tired of times being
trying!

But before you give up and stop applying, to live a life of
constant sighing (big sigh), I'll keep rhyming…

It's been said before but deems repeating, life is fleeting.
Every day you wake, you cheat the reaping, you gotta keep
reaching, no back seating, life to your fullest until you stop
beating…

See nothing changes but the date.
Life's moving forward, it's not gonna wait.
Embrace the love, forget the hate.
You gotta keep trying, it's never too late.
So keep believing, reaching and achieving,
move past those that impede proceedings,
the cheating, misleading…

They see you striving, they see you leaving
but that's on them, that's their believing.
Stop deceiving yourself from the reasons
your life's the way it is from a cause or a season.

It's your movie. What's it rated, PG-13, R or X-rated?
This game's been ending since it's begun,
so choose your path and have some fun.

You're enough.

"You're the One."

So follow your dreams and never be done.

ButwuT
SK8 BMX SNO SRF DIRT SPORT LIFE

I was gonna do that but,

well I was gonna do this but,

ButwuT

but what's stopping you from
reaching your Goals,

but what's stopping you from
attaining your Dreams?

What needs to be done?

but what are you doing?

Do something

Don't be
afraid to
speak your mind
you just might have
the clarity others are
looking for, Be heard.

I created this next one based on my dad. He was literally the stereotypical bad elderly driver. Not to mention his normal day-to-day mannerisms got me thinking of a good cartoon idea, "Senior Moment." I think it could be a nice one-panel strip somewhere if they still do that.

Yes, we love our older folks, but sometimes they say or do something that just makes us laugh, shake our heads, but still laugh. We all have our stories while hanging out with the older group, so I'm sure in some way, you can relate…

I'll never forget, one day I was standing out front, watching my dad pulling out of the driveway. As he was backing out, we noticed a UPS truck across the street, but it was a couple houses up from our house… didn't matter! Lol. My dad backed out of the driveway, across into the other lane and should of just stopped, put it in drive and went on about his day. But no, he continued to back up until he hit the UPS truck… then drove away. We couldn't believe what we just saw and just started laughing. Enjoy.

D.Butler©25

Driving is easy,..You just back up until you
hit something,..then pull forward.

Parking is easy,..You just pull forward until you
hit something,..then back up.

Senior Moment

When you're older,..
Coughing becomes an extreme sport

Oatmeal,..Lots of Oatmeal

As I sit here, looking back on my life at the "halfway" point, I realize it's just moments of time we retain, and the handful of people that mattered. So, who would I invite to watch me act like a nut on stage if I had the opportunity to spit my rhymes to a select few, a private audience. Who would I invite?

I looked back at my life so far and after forty-eight years (ehem), maybe it's just a few who, to this point in one way or another, have had a positive impact and influence in my life, and I just want to give them a nod and thank them for their presence in this journey so far.

Even though there's no rhyme here, I'm sure there could be one. Looking back at eighteen, when I just started rhyming, your first relationship, your first "love" is a memory that sticks. It's an amazing time.

Even though it's been a while, I think it would be a trip to see you in the audience. Would we still recognize each other lol? LK, my eighteen-year-old soul looks fondly back at our time. You were one of the prettiest, and I was as handsome as ever. It was a perfect time, an impressionable age. To this day, I can't drive through VF without thinking back with a smile on my face. I've always loved that place. Not to mention for whatever reason, every year on March 19th, I say "Happy Birthday" to the air; idk maybe they'll hear it. Who? Not sure who's birthday that is, but it's gotta be somebody's, right?

It's funny what the brain retains…. It was the late 80s, perfect time for exploration and first love, and through our movies and music, we really were part of the *Breakfast Club*, and we were definitely living *Some Kind of Wonderful*. Although our moment was about fifteen minutes in the story of life, I'm happy it happened and I'm glad it was you. It was such a fun time, I wish you nothing but the best kid, truly, Thanks for the memories. -xo

These next three, looking back at my life, I've had family and friends and coworkers, and I've met a lot of people, but out of everyone else in my life, putting myself out there on stage to rhyme in front of people, it's these three I would love to see in the front row in hopes of entertaining them. Jeff, Leo and Leslie, all I can think of is that you guys are three amazing souls, who even with our short, short time together, maybe five minutes in the story of our lives, gave me nothing but love and support and encouragement every time we hung out. Just. Being. Yourselves. And that was a gift from God to me. Thank you, my friends; I wish you the world…. And I hope you enjoy my rhymes. Maybe one day I'll see you up front. ;)

Tim, Coco, keeping it short and sweet. I know you might not believe in the Universe, but I've learn a lot about the Universe in my time on earth and my time with you two. Right time, right place. You two came to me at the right time, you offered help without an ask. When my life was at the bottom, you two gave me a hand up. Without knowing it, you taught me solace and showed me when you're working on yourself, there's always more to do. Thank you. I hope you like the rhymes.

Lastly, I'd like to thank my life coach, Amy Valentine. She is amazing. I was online trying to find someone who could organize my life, for a fee, almost like a silent business partner, to tell me the where to go, what to do, and when to be there kind of thing. Oh wait, I guess that's a wife, huh lolololo! That's funny.

What I found with Amy was so much more than I could of hoped for. She gave me a better understanding of the Universe, my universe and the ability to use this new perspective on my life. Yes! From her teachings is where I found my new favorite word, perspective…. She helped open the door, so I can be *Living My Best Life*. Thank you, Amy, much love for you. You give your time so others can strive. Beautiful.

If you ever have questions about your life, your choices, your path, please reach out to Amy. She may just blow your mind with a perspective you didn't see coming, which could, in turn, change your life and even your direction, with a better understanding of the Universe you're living in. Always stay open to others for clarity. You never know what you'll find.

Thank you, Amy, and all those above. It's been a trip so far, glad you were a part, hope the second half is twice as nice! Thanks for your time, hope you like my work and I'll see ya when I see ya.

Be true with your soul, not your sole purpose but your soul's purpose.

There was a time for each of us, when you were a kid in school or at work where you couldn't wait to get home to do it, whether it was a sport, a hobby, an activity or playing an instrument, etc., something that made you smile just thinking about it, where you had absolute joy and excitement about it.

It's still in you, remember it, live it, breathe it, for you are the one. Have fun and Never Be Done.

After years of asking why am I here,
today I was told and the answer was clear.

Be you, my friend, it's time to begin,
years of looking outward when it's always been within.

Your passion, your thoughts, what you create
have been your gifts from your start at the gate.

So holeshot that gate and keep on creating,
with the art from your heart, a difference you're making.

So release those dreams that I have instilled in,
for you, my friend, are one in a million.

www.ingramcontent.com/pod-product-compliance
Lightning Source LLC
Chambersburg PA
CBHW050014040726

47599CB00014B/1377